MURDER ON THE ROBOT CITY EXPRESS

THE ROBOT CITY EXPRESS: CHALLENGER FOR THE TRANS-CONTINENTAL SPEED RECORD

HARRISON: CONDUCTOR ON THE ROBOT CITY EXPRESS

GARY HORNBY: DIRECTOR OF ROBOT CITY LINES

THE ROBOT CITY ROCKET: HOLDER OF THE TRANS-CONTINENTAL SPEED RECORD

CAROLINE HEPPENHEIMER: HEART SURGEON

PROFESSOR SHIMIZU: QUANTUM PHYSICIST

PROFESSOR WADDELL: RENOWNED PHYSICIST

DIANA MCQUEEN: FILM STAR

MAX: DOG HANDLER FOR THE STARS

CHARLOTTE GRANT: FILM ACTOR

'GORGEOUS' GEORGE LEE: FILM ACTOR

STEPHEN WEST: FILM DIRECTOR

FLEETFOOT JACKSON: RO-BALL PLAYER

NATALYA ANTYUKH: RUSSIAN TENNIS PLAYER

CURT THE COFFEE ROBOT: FIRST DAY ON THE JOB

NOAH DELON: AWARD-WINNING FRENCH CHEF

LAST CALL FOR PASSENGERS BOARDING THE ROBOT CITY EXPRESS!

THAT'S IT. YOU'RE ALL CHECKED OUT AND POWERED UP NOW, EXPRESS.

THANKS, TOM. I FEEL LIKE ALL SYSTEMS ARE GO!

"IT LOOKS AS IF THE ENGINEERS HAVE FINISHED THEIR CHECKS, AND THE EXPRESS IS READY TO ROLL."

"TICKETS FOR THIS RECORD ATTEMPT SOLD OUT MONTHS AGO."

FIRST-CLASS CARRIAGES ARE IN THE MIDDLE OF THE TRAIN, SIR.

TEN MINUTES, EXPRESS. WE'RE OFF IN TEN MINUTES PRECISELY.

AND WE UNDERSTAND THAT THE ROBOT CITY ROCKET IS ON THE LINE RIGHT NOW, SENDING THE EXPRESS LUCK.

THIS IS EMMA HAMILTON FOR CHANNEL FIVE, WISHING THE EXPRESS A SAFE TRIP.

5

I'LL BE WAITING HERE IN ROBOT CITY TO WELCOME YOU, EXPRESS. REMEMBER-- KEEP YOUR SPEED UP IN THE MIDDLE SECTION AND YOU'LL BREAK THE RECORD. YOU CAN GET AWAY WITHOUT APPLYING THE BRAKES AT ALL IN THAT SECTION.

THANKS FOR THE ADVICE, ROCKET. YOUR RECORD IS A TOUGH ONE, BUT I'LL GIVE IT MY BEST SHOT.

EIGHT MINUTES TO GO! LET'S GET THE LAST PASSENGERS ON BOARD.

SAY, WHO'S THAT LATECOMER?

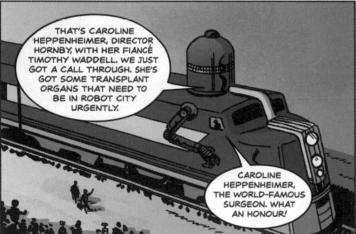

THAT'S CAROLINE HEPPENHEIMER, DIRECTOR HORNBY, WITH HER FIANCÉ TIMOTHY WADDELL. WE JUST GOT A CALL THROUGH. SHE'S GOT SOME TRANSPLANT ORGANS THAT NEED TO BE IN ROBOT CITY URGENTLY.

CAROLINE HEPPENHEIMER, THE WORLD-FAMOUS SURGEON. WHAT AN HONOUR!

TRANSPLANT ORGANS, EH? THAT'S SOME IMPORTANT CARGO!

I KNOW. I HOPE I CAN GET TO ROBOT CITY FAST ENOUGH...

YOU'RE THE FASTEST, EXPRESS!

PHEW! JUST MADE IT. THANK YOU SO MUCH FOR WAITING.

CAROLINE... WHAT A SURPRISE!

SHIMI! I DIDN'T EXPECT TO SEE YOU HERE.

OH. WADDELL. IT'S YOU.

THAT'S *PROFESSOR* WADDELL. LET'S AT LEAST BE PROFESSIONAL ABOUT THIS, PROFESSOR SHIMIZU.

IF EVERYONE'S SETTLED, I THINK WE CAN GET GOING!

PROFESSOR WADDELL, WHAT DOES IT FEEL LIKE TO BE THE SECOND-BEST PHYSICIST ON THIS TRAIN?

I WOULDN'T KNOW, PROFESSOR SHIMIZU. WHAT DOES IT FEEL LIKE TO BE DUMPED BY CAROLINE?

!!!

OKAY, TEAM, LET'S CLOSE THOSE DOORS AND GO!

HANG ON! WHAT'S ALL THE COMMOTION DOWN ON THE PLATFORM?

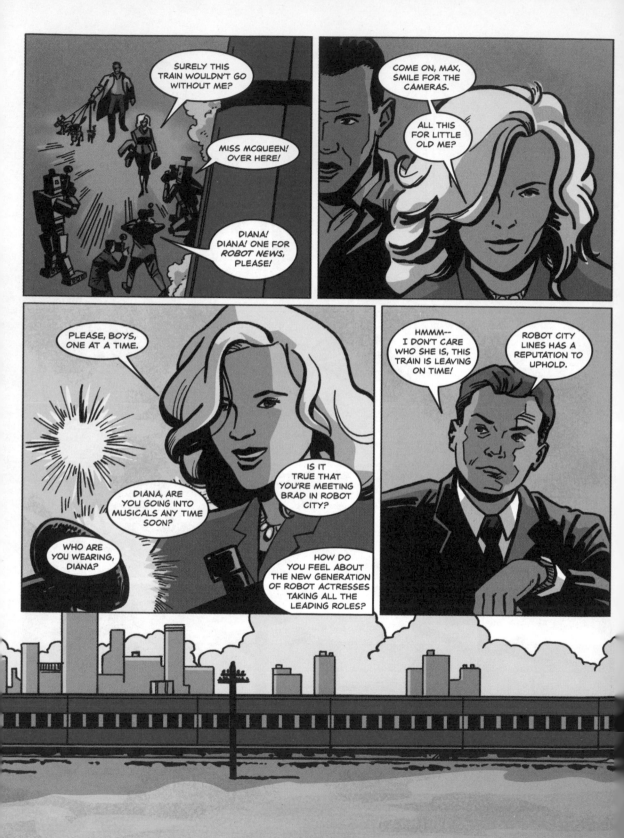

BYE, FELLAS!

GO EXPRESS! GO EXPRESS!

WOO! WOO!

GET THAT RECORD!

WOW! WOULDN'T IT BE GREAT TO BE ON THAT TRAIN?

ONE HOUR LATER IN THE FIRST-CLASS DINING CAR.

THAT'S STEPHEN WEST, THE FILM DIRECTOR! OUT OF MY WAY, TIN BOY.

STEVIE! IS THAT YOU, DARLING?

IT IS-- IT'S STEPHEN WEST!

OH NO, SHE GOT THERE FIRST, GEORGE!

DARN! I JUST WANT TO HAVE MY MEAL IN PEACE.

HERE, YOU DROPPED THIS: MURDER AT LAWRENCE GRANGE.

THANK YOU, PROFESSOR. I WAS JUST GETTING INTO THAT. LET ME SHOW YOU TO YOUR TABLE.

ACTUALLY, I'M NOT REALLY IN THE MOOD FOR PEOPLE TONIGHT. I THINK I'LL JUST GO BACK AND EAT IN MY CABIN.

OH! EXCUSE ME--

HI!

SHIMI... IT'S GOOD TO SEE YOU, BUT YOU'VE GOT TO LET IT GO NOW.

I'M MARRYING TIMOTHY NEXT MONTH, AND WE CAN'T KEEP HAVING THESE... AWKWARD MOMENTS.

INDEED.

OOOF!

OH, CAREFUL NOW, SIR! THAT MUST HAVE HURT!

JACKSON! WATCH WHERE YOU GO!

I ALWAYS SEEM TO BE IN THE WRONG PLACE AT THE WRONG TIME.

PLEASE, ARE YOU ALL RIGHT? MY BOYFRIEND IS BIG AMERICAN ROBOT... A BIT CLUMSY, NO? BUT HE DOES NOT MEAN TO PUSH YOU OUT OF WAY.

OH YES, SIR. I'M SORRY. I'M ALL NUTS AND BOLTS TODAY.

IT'S FINE. IT'S NOT YOUR FAULT. I'M JUST A BIT... UNWELL.

WON'T YOU JOIN US FOR SOMETHING TO EAT? WE'RE JUST HEADING TO THE DINING CAR.

THANK YOU, BUT I'M HEADING BACK TO MY CABIN. I JUST WANT TO BE ALONE.

I'LL CALL ONE OF THE RESTAURANT ROBOTS TO TAKE MY ORDER.

HELLO, SIR. I'M CURT THE COFFEE ROBOT. IT IS MY PLEASURE TO SERVE YOU TODAY.

IT'S MY FIRST DAY ON THE JOB, SIR. I'M A BIT NERVOUS, BUT I HOPE I CAN STILL SERVE YOU WELL.

DON'T WORRY, YOU'RE DOING FINE. I'M SURE YOU'RE AN EXCELLENT COFFEE ROBOT. NOW, I'D LIKE TO ORDER A CAESAR SALAD, PLEASE.

THANK YOU VERY MUCH, SIR. I'LL HAVE THE CHEF PREPARE YOUR MEAL RIGHT AWAY.

GOOD. THEN I CAN EAT IT HERE... BY MYSELF.

STOP THE TRAIN? ARE YOU MAD, HARRISON?

THIS IS A RECORD ATTEMPT!

NOT EVEN A DEAD PHYSICIST IS GOING TO STOP THE EXPRESS!

BUT, SIR, WE MUST STOP. IT LOOKS LIKE HE WAS MURDERED!

THERE'S NOTHING TO PROVE THAT. THE PROFESSOR MIGHT HAVE TRASHED HIS OWN ROOM, LOOKING FOR HIS... GLASSES. ANYWAY, ROBOT CITY PD HAVE THE BEST MURDER DEPARTMENT IN THE COUNTRY. WE'LL RADIO AHEAD TO LET THEM KNOW WE'RE COMING, BUT WE'RE NOT STOPPING THIS TRAIN.

IF THE EXPRESS CAN BREAK THAT RECORD, ROBOT CITY LINES MIGHT STILL BE ABLE TO COME OUT OF THIS UNTARNISHED...

ANYWAY, YOU'RE ALWAYS READING MURDER MYSTERIES, AREN'T YOU?

OH, YES. I LOVE THEM. I MUST HAVE READ OVER A HUNDRED. SPRINGLOCK HOLMES IS MY FAVOURITE.

IN THAT CASE, HARRISON, YOU CAN INVESTIGATE THE PROFESSOR'S DEATH. FIND OUT WHAT HAPPENED BY THE TIME THIS TRAIN ROLLS INTO ROBOT CITY.

THE FUTURE OF ROBOT CITY LINES DEPENDS ON YOU.

GULP!

B-B-BUT--

NO IFS, NO BUTS. JUST GET RESULTS, HARRISON, OR YOU MIGHT BE RECYCLED!

SCHOOOOM!

SO, THE FATE OF ROBOT CITY LINES IS IN MY HANDS. GOODNESS! WHERE TO BEGIN? CONCENTRATE, HARRISON--WHAT WOULD SPRINGLOCK HOLMES DO?

LET'S BE SYSTEMATIC. I AM A ROBOT, AFTER ALL!

I'LL START BY SEARCHING PROFESSOR SHIMIZU'S CABIN. THEN I NEED TO INTERVIEW THE OTHER PASSENGERS. YES, THAT'S IT. COME ON, HARRISON. KEEP CALM!

INTERVIEW 1:
HEAD CHEF
NOAH DELON
TIME: 10:00 P.M.

MAIS OUI, I HAVE MET THIS SHIMIZU BEFORE. ONCE THIS MAN-- THIS PROFESSOR--HE ATE AT MY RESTAURANT AND HE SENT BACK HIS MAIN COURSE! HE SAID IT WAS COLD, THAT IT WAS NOT COOKED! IMBÉCILE!

AND WAS IT COOKED?

THE JUNIOR CHEF HAD NOT COOKED IT PROPERLY. I INSTANTLY DISMANTLED HIM. HE WAS FAULTY--BAD CIRCUITS.

BUT NO ONE, MAN OR ROBOT, SENDS ANYTHING BACK TO NOAH DELON'S KITCHEN. YOU CANNOT IMAGINE HOW I FELT. I WAS SO... ANGRY.

ANGRY ENOUGH TO POISON HIM WHEN HE ORDERED A MEAL ON THIS TRAIN?

WHAT? NON! YOU KNOW WHAT I DO? I SAY TO MYSELF: NOAH, YOU ARE THE GREATEST CHEF EVER TO COOK ON THE RAILROADS.

I SAY, D'ACCORD PROFESSEUR, I WILL COOK THE MOST DELICIOUS MEAL YOU HAVE EVER EATEN. YOU WILL NEVER HAVE TASTED A CAESAR SALAD LIKE THIS BEFORE. IT WILL BE SOMETHING TO... TO...

DIE FOR?

NON! TO REMEMBER FOR THE REST OF YOUR LIFE.

AWOOOWOOO!

INTERVIEW 2: CAROLINE HEPPENHEIMER AND PROFESSOR WADDELL TIME: 10:30 P.M. TELL ME ABOUT YOUR RELATIONSHIP WITH PROFESSOR SHIMIZU. WEREN'T YOU ENGAGED AT ONE TIME?

WE WERE.

BUT NEITHER OF US COULD FIND THE TIME IN OUR BUSY LIVES TO SET A WEDDING DATE. FOR BOTH OF US, OUR WORK WAS MORE IMPORTANT. WE AGREED TO CALL IT OFF.

BUT HE STILL HAD FEELINGS FOR YOU? I SAW THE MEETING IN THE DINING CAR. WERE THOSE FEELINGS MUTUAL?

WELL, I STILL CARE ABOUT HIM-- SOB--THAT'S CARED NOW, ISN'T IT?

DARLING, YOU DON'T HAVE TO ANSWER THESE QUESTIONS.

NO, IT'S ALL RIGHT. AFTER WE CALLED THE WEDDING OFF, WE WENT OUR SEPARATE WAYS. THAT'S WHEN I MET TIMOTHY. IT WAS A CASE OF THE RIGHT MAN AT THE RIGHT TIME.

BUT ALTHOUGH I HAD MOVED ON FROM SHIMI, HE HADN'T MOVED ON, AND I KEPT GETTING LETTERS AND CALLS. AFTER A WHILE, I HAD TO TELL HIM TO STOP. I HAD TO TELL HIM I DIDN'T LOVE HIM ANY MORE.

THAT'S NOT STRICTLY TRUE, IS IT, DR HEPPENHEIMER?

WHAT--WHAT ARE YOU IMPLYING?

WELL, PROFESSOR WADDELL, YOUR FIANCÉE WAS STILL WRITING TO PROFESSOR SHIMIZU AS RECENTLY AS TWO MONTHS AGO. I FOUND THESE LETTERS IN HIS LUGGAGE.

OH, NO!

AND YOU, PROFESSOR WADDELL. YOU KNEW SHIMIZU ALSO.

YES. WE WERE BOTH PHYSICISTS.

AND BITTER RIVALS, FROM WHAT I'VE READ.

WE DISAGREED ABOUT A NUMBER OF THINGS, BUT MOSTLY HE COULDN'T STAND ME BECAUSE CAROLINE CHOSE ME INSTEAD OF HIM.

THE MAN WAS CONSUMED WITH JEALOUSY. EVERY TIME WE MET HE WAS INSUFFERABLE. HE DROVE ME MAD.

MAD ENOUGH TO MURDER HIM?

NO, OF COURSE NOT!

SCHWOOSH

INTERVIEW 3: DIANA MCQUEEN AND HER DOG HANDLER, MAX TIME: 11:15 P.M.

YOU LOOK VERY ELEGANT, MISS MCQUEEN.

WHY, THANK YOU. I LIKE TO MAKE THE EFFORT FOR ALL MY FANS. THEY DO SO ENJOY TO SEE ME LOOKING MY BEST AT ALL TIMES.

INDEED. I NOTICE YOU HAVE SOME BEAUTIFUL JEWELLERY ON TODAY.

YES, I LOVE MY JEWELS.

THEN, PERHAPS YOU KNEW ABOUT PROFESSOR SHIMIZU'S FAMOUS DIAMONDS? HE WAS STUDYING THEM ON A QUANTUM LEVEL AND HAD QUITE AN EXTENSIVE COLLECTION.

I'D HEARD ABOUT THEM, YES.

WERE YOU AWARE THAT HE WAS ON HIS WAY TO ROBOT CITY TO DELIVER HIS FAMOUS RUSSIAN DIAMOND TO THE RUSSIAN EMBASSY?

OF COURSE NOT. I DIDN'T EVEN KNOW THE MAN.

INTERESTING. THEN HOW DO YOU EXPLAIN THE MESSAGE FROM YOU THAT I FOUND ON HIS MOBILE PHONE? YOU ASKED IF HE WOULD SELL YOU THE DIAMOND INSTEAD OF TAKING IT TO THE EMBASSY.

OH. YOU SAW THAT, DID YOU?

SO PERHAPS YOU CAN TELL US WHERE THE RUSSIAN DIAMOND IS? IT WAS MISSING FROM ITS CASE IN SHIMIZU'S LUGGAGE.

HURRMPH!

I REALLY HAVE NO IDEA WHAT YOU'RE GETTING AT. NOW, IF YOU DON'T MIND, I HAVE SOME FAN MAIL TO ANSWER, SO I'LL LEAVE YOU TO YOUR... CONDUCTING!

SCHWISHH!

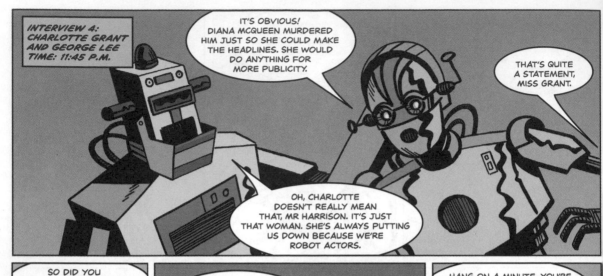

IT'S OBVIOUS! DIANA MCQUEEN MURDERED HIM JUST SO SHE COULD MAKE THE HEADLINES. SHE WOULD DO ANYTHING FOR MORE PUBLICITY.

THAT'S QUITE A STATEMENT, MISS GRANT.

OH, CHARLOTTE DOESN'T REALLY MEAN THAT, MR HARRISON. IT'S JUST THAT WOMAN. SHE'S ALWAYS PUTTING US DOWN BECAUSE WE'RE ROBOT ACTORS.

SO DID YOU MEET PROFESSOR SHIMIZU ON THE EXPRESS?

NO, WE ONLY SAW HIM FROM AFAR. GEORGE POINTED HIM OUT AS HE GOT ON BOARD.

HANG ON A MINUTE. YOU'RE SAYING YOU RECOGNISED A PHYSICIST, FROM SOME DISTANCE, GETTING ON BOARD A BUSY TRAIN?

NOT MANY PEOPLE WOULD RECOGNISE A PHYSICIST-- UNLESS THEY'D MET HIM BEFORE, OF COURSE. HAD YOU MET THE PROFESSOR BEFORE, MR LEE?

WELL, UM, YEAH. I MET HIM LAST YEAR. HE WAS ONE OF THE FINANCIAL BACKERS ON *RIVERS OF RUST*, A MOVIE I WROTE.

GEORGE, HONEY, DON'T. YOU'LL GET ALL UPSET AGAIN. YOU'LL OVERHEAT!

RIVERS OF RUST? I'VE NEVER HEARD OF IT.

IF YOU MUST KNOW, IT DIDN'T GO AHEAD. THE BACKERS PULLED OUT IN THE END. THEY SAID MY SCRIPT WAS TOO WEAK.

I SEE. SO YOUR FILM GOT CANNED. AND HOW DID THAT MAKE YOU FEEL, MR LEE?

I WASN'T TOO HAPPY, TO BE HONEST WITH YOU. THAT SCRIPT WAS MY MASTERPIECE.

I'M FED UP WITH BEING AN ACTOR AND ALWAYS BEING TOLD WHAT TO DO. THIS WAS MY CHANCE TO BE THE BOSS-- A CREATIVE FORCE!

SO BECAUSE THE PROFESSOR WITHDREW HIS INVESTMENT, YOUR DREAM NEVER BECAME A REALITY?

HANG ON A SECOND. WHAT ARE YOU GETTING AT? I MEAN, IT WASN'T JUST THE PROFESSOR WHO PULLED OUT. I'M NOT SURE I LIKE WHAT YOU'RE IMPLYING...

GEORGE, DEAR, CALM DOWN. I'M SURE HE'S JUST DOING HIS JOB.

WELL, THANKS FOR YOUR TIME. IT'S BEEN MOST ENLIGHTENING.

ZOOM!

INTERVIEW 5: SPORTS STARS FLEETFOOT JACKSON AND NATALYA ANTYUKH TIME: 12:20 A.M.

I DIDN'T MEAN TO RUN INTO HIM. IT WAS AN ACCIDENT. I'M A BIT NERVOUS ABOUT MY TRY-OUT FOR THE ROBOT CITY DYNAMOS. I HAVEN'T BEEN ABLE TO CONTROL MY CIRCUITS ALL DAY. I JUST BUMPED HIM. I'M SURE I DIDN'T HURT HIM.

JUST LIKE YOU WERE SURE YOU DIDN'T KNOCK THE HEAD OFF THE METAL MARAUDERS' NUMBER TWO LAST SEASON?

THAT WAS AN ACCIDENT! THE REPLAY SHOWED IT WAS HIS FAULT. HE BUMPED INTO ME!

THEY FOUND OUT AFTERWARDS THAT HE'D HAD HIS HEAD LOOSENED ON PURPOSE. THE MARAUDERS FAKED IT SO THEY COULD GET A PENALTY SHOT! BESIDES, HE'S FINE NOW. THEY PUT HIS HEAD BACK ON.

BACKWARDS!

HE LOOKS BETTER THAT WAY.

WELL, IT'S TRUE! COME ON, AM I THE ONLY ONE WHO THINKS IT'S AN IMPROVEMENT?

NOW, MISS ANTYUKH, YOU'RE FROM SAINT PETERSBURG?

YES. THAT IS WHERE I WAS MADE. IT IS A BEAUTIFUL CITY.

HOME OF THE RUSSIAN DIAMOND, I BELIEVE...

UNTIL IT WAS STOLEN IN WORLD WAR TWO. LIKE ALL OF RUSSIA I WOULD LIKE TO SEE THIS FAMOUS JEWEL RETURNED TO OUR GREAT MUSEUM, THE HERMITAGE.

YES, I REMEMBER YOU TALKING ABOUT IT DURING AN INTERVIEW AT LAST YEAR'S ROBOT CITY TENNIS TOURNAMENT. A BIT OF A COINCIDENCE, THEN, THAT PROFESSOR SHIMIZU HAD THE DIAMOND WITH HIM ON THIS JOURNEY?

I DO NOT KNOW ABOUT THAT. I AM JUST TENNIS PLAYER.

I'M ON MY WAY TO ROBOT CITY TO TALK TO CHARLTON 68 ABOUT A NEW JET JEFFERSON MOVIE.

INTERVIEW 6: STEPHEN WEST, FILM DIRECTOR TIME: 1:55 A.M.

ANOTHER JET JEFFERSON MOVIE? WOW, THAT MUST BE THE THIRD IN, WHAT IS IT? TWO YEARS?

WELL, THOSE MOVIES PUT BREAD ON THE TABLE, SO TO SPEAK. WE ALL HAVE TO EARN A LIVING.

ARE YOU HAVING FINANCIAL DIFFICULTIES, MR WEST?

WELL, I'VE BEEN UNLUCKY WITH SOME INVESTMENTS RECENTLY, BUT I'LL BOUNCE BACK.

I'VE NOTICED THAT YOU'VE BEEN KEEPING RATHER A LOW PROFILE ON THIS TRIP. WHY IS THAT?

TO TELL YOU THE TRUTH, THERE ARE SOME ACTORS ON BOARD WHO KEEP PESTERING ME.

DIANA MCQUEEN IS A PRIMA DONNA, AND GEORGE LEE AND CHARLOTTE GRANT ARE SUCH HANGERS-ON. THEY'RE ALWAYS TRYING TO WHEEDLE THEIR WAY INTO MY NEXT MOVIE. SOMETIMES THEY SEEM PRETTY DESPERATE.

SO THEY'D DO ANYTHING FOR YOU?

I SUPPOSE YOU COULD PUT IT LIKE THAT.

MAYBE EVEN COMMIT A MURDER TO STEAL A VALUABLE DIAMOND... IF YOU ASKED THEM?

HEY, CAREFUL NOW. BUT I LIKE YOUR ANGLE-- YOU'RE A SHARP ROBOT.

WELL, I WON'T TAKE UP ANY MORE OF YOUR TIME FOR NOW. THANK YOU, SIR.

SURE. NO PROBLEM.

WHOOOSH!

HOW'S IT GOING, HARRISON?

A LOT OF THEM SEEM TO HAVE A MOTIVE, MR HORNBY. IT'S A REAL CONUNDRUM.

EXCUSE ME, EXCUSE ME!

WELL, IT'S A CONUNDRUM THAT NEEDS SOLVING BEFORE WE GET TO ROBOT CITY. IF YOU PULL THIS OFF, YOU'LL HAVE A BRIGHT FUTURE AT ROBOT CITY LINES. IF NOT...

YES, CURT, WHAT IS IT?

I DID IT! IT WAS ME! MY COFFEE WAS TOO STRONG. IT POISONED HIM. I KILLED HIM. MY FIRST DAY WORKING ON THE ROBOT CITY EXPRESS AND I'VE KILLED A PASSENGER!

I DON'T DESERVE THIS JOB. I'M NOT WORTHY OF SERVING MANY TYPES OF COFFEE FROM AROUND THE WORLD AND ALSO OTHER HOT BEVERAGES TO THE PASSENGERS.

I SHOULD BE DECOMMISSIONED. AT THE LEAST I'LL HAVE TO RESIGN FROM THE ROBOT CITY COFFEE CLUB!

NOW, NOW. PROFESSOR SHIMIZU'S COFFEE CUP WAS STILL FULL. HE HADN'T TOUCHED IT. YOU DIDN'T KILL HIM.

OH, THANK HEAVENS! THAT'S SUCH A RELIEF. I FELT QUITE FAINT WITH ALL THE WORRY.

YES, OF COURSE. HERE, SIT DOWN. CAN I GET YOU A CUP OF COFFEE?

THANK YOU. ACTUALLY, I'M NOT MUCH OF A COFFEE DRINKER.

NOW, TELL ME HOW PROFESSOR SHIMIZU LOOKED WHEN YOU SAW HIM LAST.

COME IN, HARRISON!

HARRISON, HAVE YOU CRACKED THE CASE YET?

NOT YET, EXPRESS. ACTUALLY, I COULD DO WITH SOME HELP, PLEASE.

PROFESSOR SHIMIZU'S CABIN. EARLY NEXT MORNING.

HMMMN. MOST INTERESTING.

THIS SEAL IS UNBROKEN. THESE PILLS HAVEN'T BEEN OPENED!

COME IN, HARRISON.

MORNING, EXPRESS.

I'VE JUST HAD A MESSAGE FROM PROFESSOR SHIMIZU'S PERSONAL PHYSICIAN WITH THE INFORMATION YOU REQUESTED. I'VE ALSO HAD ONE FROM INTERPOL AND THE HERMITAGE MUSEUM. I'LL FORWARD THEM TO YOU RIGHT NOW.

STAND BY. HERE THEY COME.

THANKS, EXPRESS. ARE YOU STILL ON COURSE FOR THE RECORD?

I HAVE DISCOVERED THAT SOME OF YOU HAVE MORE REASON THAN OTHERS TO WANT PROFESSOR SHIMIZU OUT OF THE WAY!

REASONS TO MURDER HIM, HARRISON?

NOT NECESSARILY, DIRECTOR HORNBY. BUT NOT EVERYONE HERE IS EXACTLY WHO THEY SAY THEY ARE.

REALLY? DO CONTINUE.

YOU, MISS ANTYUKH-- AS WELL AS BEING AN INTERNATIONALLY FAMOUS TENNIS PLAYER, YOU HAVE ANOTHER JOB, DON'T YOU?

WHAT ARE YOU SAYING? EVERYONE KNOWS I AM TOP STAR OF TENNIS. I DO NOT HAVE ANY SPARE TIME FOR OTHER JOBS!

I HAVE TALKED WITH THE HERMITAGE.

OKAY, OKAY! IT'S TRUE. I ALSO AM INTERNATIONAL AGENT FOR THE HERMITAGE MUSEUM IN SAINT PETERSBURG.

PROFESSOR SHIMIZU HAD AGREED TO RETURN THE RUSSIAN DIAMOND TO ITS RIGHTFUL HOME IN SAINT PETERSBURG.

HE WAS GOING TO VISIT THE RUSSIAN EMBASSY IN ROBOT CITY AND HAND IT OVER. MY JOB WAS TO WATCH THE PROFESSOR AND MAKE SURE HE DID AS HE PROMISED, RETURNING THE DIAMOND SAFELY. I DID NOT DO A GOOD JOB, DID I?

NOW, NOW, NATALYA DARLIN'. NO ONE COULD HAVE GUESSED THAT THE PROFESSOR WOULD BE POISONED ON THE TRAIN...

POISONED? SO I DID KILL HIM WITH MY COFFEE?!

NO, DON'T WORRY, CURT. AS I SAID, HE HADN'T DRUNK ANY OF HIS COFFEE AND, IN FACT, NEITHER HAD HE EATEN ANY OF HIS MEAL.

SO BASICALLY YOU'RE SAYING HE WASN'T KILLED BY EITHER THE CHEF OR THE COFFEE ROBOT.

FORMIDABLE! NOW NOBODY CAN SAY THEY DIED FROM MY FOOD AND THEY WON'T BE TAKING MY RESTAURANT STARS!

INDEED, YOU'RE BOTH INNOCENT.

BUT IF HE WASN'T POISONED, HOW WAS HE MURDERED?

HE WASN'T MURDERED AT ALL! BUT IF ANYONE CAN BE SAID TO HAVE KILLED HIM, IT WOULD BE YOU, DR HEPPENHEIMER.

YOU'D BETTER KNOW WHERE YOU'RE GOING WITH THIS, HARRISON...

GOOD HEAVENS, WHAT IS HE GETTING AT?

PROFESSOR SHIMIZU HAD A VERY BAD HEART CONDITION. ALTHOUGH HE WAS CARRYING THE RUSSIAN DIAMOND WITH HIM, THE MAIN REASON FOR HIS VISIT TO ROBOT CITY WAS TO SEE A HEART SPECIALIST.

APPARENTLY, HIS CONDITION BEGAN TO DETERIORATE DRAMATICALLY TWO MONTHS AGO. CAN YOU GUESS THE REASON FOR THAT, DR HEPPENHEIMER?

YES... WE HAD BEEN TALKING TO EACH OTHER ABOUT GETTING BACK TOGETHER, AS YOU WELL KNOW IF YOU'VE READ THOSE PRIVATE LETTERS. BUT YOU'LL ALSO KNOW THAT I DECIDED I COULDN'T DO IT. I LOVE TIMOTHY. TWO MONTHS AGO, I FINISHED IT FOR GOOD.

HE WASN'T EXPECTING TO SEE YOU ON THE TRAIN. MEETING YOU PUSHED HIM OVER THE EDGE. I FOUND HIS HEART TABLETS. HE HADN'T TAKEN ANY OF THEM, ALMOST AS THOUGH HE HAD JUST GIVEN UP.

SO HE DIED... OF A BROKEN HEART?

YES, DIRECTOR HORNBY. I BELIEVE SO.

PHEW! I MEAN, HOW TERRIBLE.

A BROKEN HEART.

I'VE BEEN ADVISED BY HIS PHYSICIAN THAT IT COULD HAVE HAPPENED AT ANY TIME.

HANG ON A SECOND. IF HE WASN'T MURDERED AND HE JUST DIED OF NATURAL CAUSES, THEN HOW COME HE WAS ROBBED?

YES, I HEARD ALL HIS PAPERS HAD BEEN STOLEN.

I HEARD THAT HIS MONEY WAS TAKEN AS WELL.

ACTUALLY, HIS PAPERS AND HIS MONEY WEREN'T STOLEN.

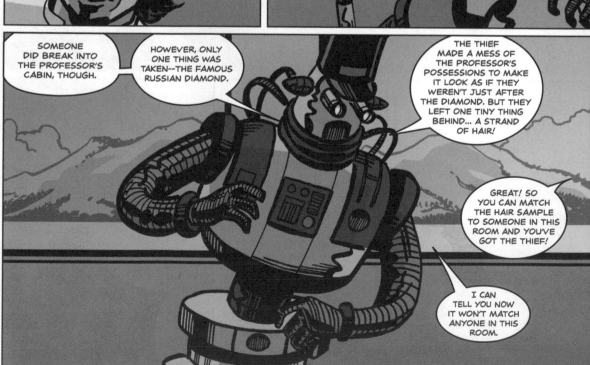

SOMEONE DID BREAK INTO THE PROFESSOR'S CABIN, THOUGH.

HOWEVER, ONLY ONE THING WAS TAKEN--THE FAMOUS RUSSIAN DIAMOND.

THE THIEF MADE A MESS OF THE PROFESSOR'S POSSESSIONS TO MAKE IT LOOK AS IF THEY WEREN'T JUST AFTER THE DIAMOND. BUT THEY LEFT ONE TINY THING BEHIND... A STRAND OF HAIR!

GREAT! SO YOU CAN MATCH THE HAIR SAMPLE TO SOMEONE IN THIS ROOM AND YOU'VE GOT THE THIEF!

I CAN TELL YOU NOW IT WON'T MATCH ANYONE IN THIS ROOM.

HE'S GOING FOR THE ROOF!

NATALYA, I'M GONNA STOP HIM AND GET THAT RUSSIAN DIAMOND BACK FOR YOU!

BE CAREFUL, JACKSON. THE TRAIN GOES VERY FAST!

DON'T WORRY, THEY DON'T CALL ME 'FLEETFOOT' FOR NOTHING.

MCKENZIE! GIVE YOURSELF UP! YOU CAN'T OUTPACE ME.

GOOD GRIEF! HARRISON, WHAT'S GOING ON? THERE ARE TWO PASSENGERS RUNNING ALONG MY ROOF!

THWACK!

GET BACK! WHY WON'T YOU JUST LEAVE ME ALONE?

MISSED ME, BUT YOU BROKE PART OF THE EXPRESS!

WHOA! THAT CONNECTED!

LET'S PUT A STOP TO THIS RIGHT NOW!

AAARGH! MY HEAD-- DON'T RIP OFF MY HEAD!

HOW MANY TIMES DO I HAVE TO SAY IT? THAT INCIDENT WITH THE MARAUDERS WASN'T MY FAULT!

JUST DON'T TOUCH MY HEAD!

UH-OH! SOMETHING'S WRONG...

GOT YA! I THINK THE ROBOT CITY POLICE WILL BE VERY INTERESTED IN YOU.

AND NATALYA IS GOING TO BE VERY INTERESTED IN THIS--THE RUSSIAN DIAMOND.

ATTENTION, CREW! WE'VE GOT A BIT OF A SITUATION HERE.

MY BRAKING SYSTEMS AREN'T WORKING. THEY MUST HAVE BEEN DAMAGED WHEN THE GUYS FELL THROUGH THE HATCH.

THAT'S NOT THE WORST OF IT, EXPRESS: YOU'VE BLOWN A LOT OF SYSTEMS TRYING TO SLOW DOWN!

EXPRESS? WHAT'S HAPPENING? YOU SEEM TO BE PICKING UP AN AWFUL LOT OF SPEED!

HARRISON, YOU'VE GOT TO GET EVERYONE TO THE BACK OF THE TRAIN!
MCKENZIE AND FLEETFOOT DAMAGED SOME IMPORTANT SYSTEMS WHILE THEY WERE FIGHTING AND SOME OF MY EMERGENCY BACK-UPS HAVE FAILED. WHAT'S MORE...

WE'RE ON THE OUTSKIRTS OF ROBOT CITY, BUT *I CAN'T STOP!*

IT'S NOT GOING TO BE LONG BEFORE WE RUN OUT OF TRACK!

ADJUST YOUR SPEED SLIGHTLY, ROCKET.

THAT'S IT— I'M CLOSING IN NOW!

CENTRAL STATION, THEY'RE STILL COMING IN FAST! STAND BY, CRASH TEAM.

SCREEEECH!

WE'RE SLOWING DOWN, BUT IT COULD STILL BE MESSY!

I'VE NOT PRACTISED MY CONTROLLED CRASHING FOR A WHILE...

THIS IS IT! WE'RE GOING IN!

SCREEEEE!

HOLD ON TO YOUR HATS, EVERYONE.

HERE THEY COME. STAND BY, RESCUE TEAMS!

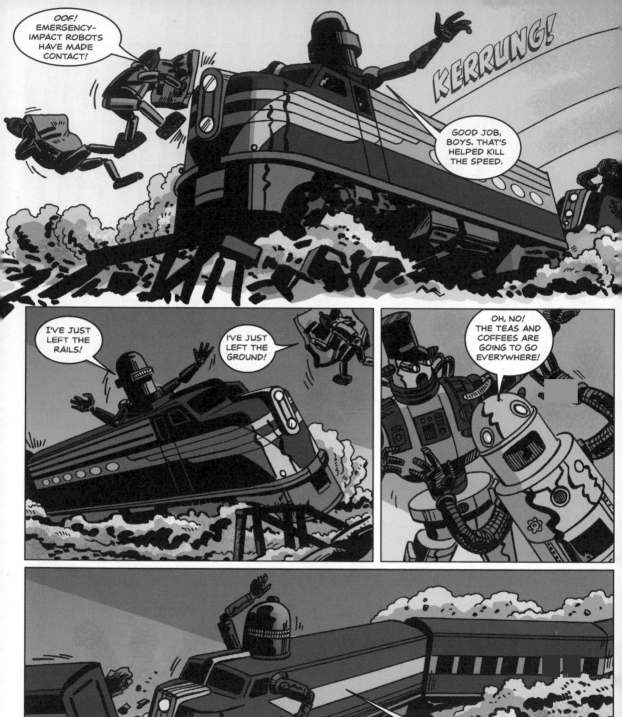

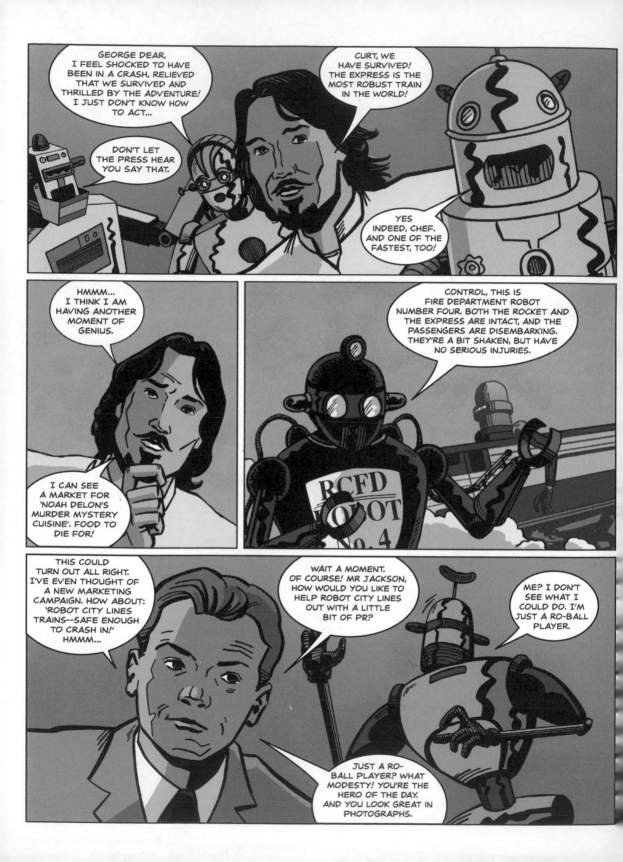

THE END

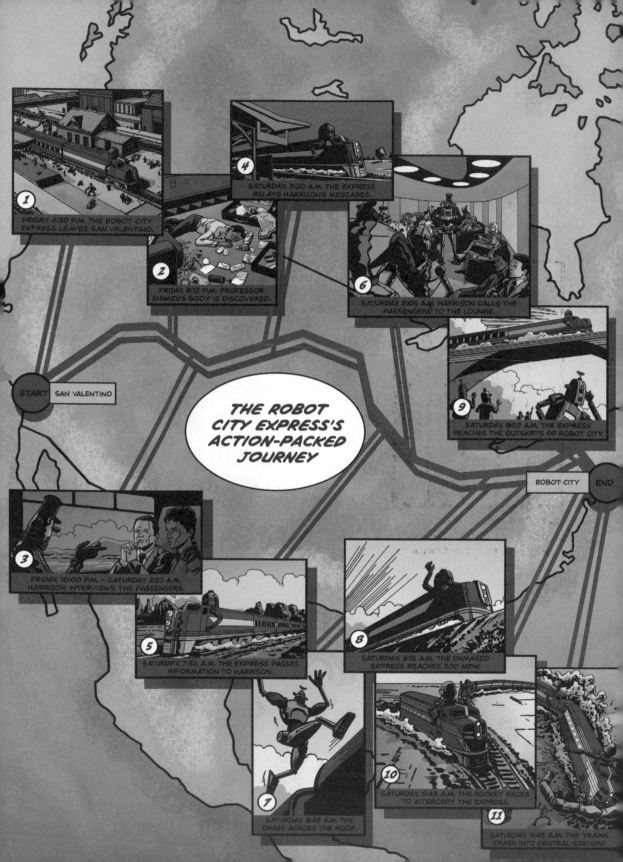

THE ROBOT CITY EXPRESS'S ACTION-PACKED JOURNEY

START · SAN VALENTINO

ROBOT CITY · END

1. FRIDAY, 4:30 P.M. THE ROBOT CITY EXPRESS LEAVES SAN VALENTINO.

2. FRIDAY, 8:12 P.M. PROFESSOR SHIMIZU'S BODY IS DISCOVERED.

3. FRIDAY, 10:00 P.M. – SATURDAY, 2:20 A.M. HARRISON INTERVIEWS THE PASSENGERS.

4. SATURDAY, 3:00 A.M. THE EXPRESS RELAYS HARRISON'S MESSAGES.

5. SATURDAY, 7:52 A.M. THE EXPRESS PASSES INFORMATION TO HARRISON.

6. SATURDAY, 8:05 A.M. HARRISON CALLS THE PASSENGERS TO THE LOUNGE.

7. SATURDAY, 8:48 A.M. THE CHASE ACROSS THE ROOF.

8. SATURDAY, 9:15 A.M. THE DAMAGED EXPRESS REACHES 300 MPH!

9. SATURDAY, 9:29 A.M. THE EXPRESS REACHES THE OUTSKIRTS OF ROBOT CITY.

10. SATURDAY, 9:43 A.M. THE ROCKET RACES TO INTERCEPT THE EXPRESS.

11. SATURDAY, 9:45 A.M. THE TRAINS CRASH INTO CENTRAL STATION!